Dear

With
all you have achieved.

A New Day

Words of hope and inspiration

Dianne M. Tarpy
Author of *From the Heart*

Blessings,

Dianne M. Tarpy

5-17-22

First Edition

Book 2 - The series *From the Heart*

Book cover and interior formatting by
SusanasBooks LLC

From the Heart art - Haley Althea Phillips

Photographs and artists are listed under Credits.

Published by Bradford Beech Tree Publishing
The United States of America.

Diannemtarpyauthor.com
From the Heart – Diannemtarpy – Facebook
Diannemtarpyauthor - Instagram
All rights reserved.
Print ISBN: 978-1-7366332-1-2

#fromtheheart

Dianne Tarpy: Featured Poet of
Week 10

Author Tia B.

EDITOR, POET, PUBLISHER

Dedication

This book is dedicated to you. As you hold it in your hands, know that the words you read are for and because of you. How thankful I am you are here!

These words flow from my mind and my heart, influenced greatly by what is happening in this time of uncertainty, during the year of 2020, in our homes and our world.

I write to inspire, to give hope, and to help make the days easier. About the things that we celebrate, mourn, work through or delight in. As you read each page, it is my hope that the writings make a difference in your lives, spur on a thought, provoke a feeling, or encourage you to take action.

The intent is to illustrate we are often affected by the same things; that our shortcomings or our successes are often similar; that the differences between us are often smaller than we think.

To all of you who are along for the ride: I am grateful. I am so happy that my words resonate with you!

Know that these words, carefully placed on the page, are written from the heart, on this new day, especially for you.

Contents

Foreword

I was so thrilled when I heard that Dianne would be publishing a second book of her beautiful poetry. This world has collectively suffered so much over the past year with the pandemic and one thing we all surely need is something inspirational and uplifting to carry us forward.

Dianne's words are just that! They lift us up and inspire us to not give up. Her words also serve to stir in us the desire to pause, reflect and to see if we can go deeper into our hearts and feel gratitude for things both big and small. The daily devotional style is wonderful because you can just pick a page and start your day off on the right path. And if you ever want to challenge yourself to try something new, I promise you, her words will build you up enough to go for it!

Thank you, Dianne for sharing your gifts with the world at a time when we need it most.

Carolyn Coppola, author *Minivans, Meltdowns & Merlot.*

I had the pleasure of interviewing Dianne on a recent *Three Guys Podcast* episode. Her writings of hope, inspiration and purpose align with the foundational intent of our podcast. Dianne´s words paint amazing emotional and mental photographs.

She has the ability to bring her written word to life on the page, which in turn provides a lift to readers.

I start each day by reading her poetry for the motivation it offers, which helps to make my day a success.

Brian Nazarian, *The Three Guys Podcast*
https://linktr.ee/thethreeguyspodcast

Once again, Dianne has written poems that fill the heart and mind with joy – the joy of being alive. I'm proud to be a small part of bringing this second anthology to our friends worldwide. I know we will keep this book handy. Mine will be by my favorite chair, knowing the poems are always there, waiting for me when I need them the most.

Susana Jiménez-Mueller, Author and Podcaster
Now I Swim – Ahora yo Nado- A memoir
The Green Plantain - The Cuban Stories Project Podcast
https://www.susanasbooks.com

Preface

I wrote daily during the year of 2020, as the Covid 19 pandemic surged and affected our neighborhoods and our world. Often, I sat looking out my window wondering what the new day would bring. Each day I posted my words on social media, and was in awe of the positive response. Soon I realized I had enough poems to fill a series of books; hence, A New Day came about as the second book in the series of *From the Heart*.

It was a year of uncertainty when the isolation we experienced provided more solitary time than ever before. Writing became my answer of what to do during these periods of solitude. I found that we were all united in this time of isolation, even though we were apart. My first book was so well received by people that it gave me all the confidence needed to move forward. The time was right for poetry, as many were seeking ways to better understand what was going on during these long days. Poetry gave us a vehicle for understanding and a mechanism to cope.

This series is intended to soothe the soul and the heart of the reader and bring them to a place where hope continues to lead the way. Further, to help them believe in themselves and their ability to cope with the disappointments that life often brings.

These words have a theme, as the chapter headings indicate. Often, it is the turning points of life that draw us to poetry. The right poem, when read at exactly the right time, helps to makes sense of our experiences.

My hope is that whether you read one poem a day or all 70 in one sitting, that you will find words that make sense of your experiences and hit home for you.

Dianne M. Tarpy
Haverhill, Massachusetts
July 3, 2021

Acknowledgments

To my extended group of family and friends, led by the entire Tarpy/Beckford tribe, my heartfelt thanks. Your true love, respect and support provided me with the inspiration I needed, on good days and bad, which allowed these words to flow.

Special thanks to my husband Jim and children Gregg, Eric and Melissa, along with their families. To my "Great 8" grandchildren, Alek, Tess, Shea, Tyler, Megg, Kyle, Haley, and Lilly, I adore you. Each of you, in your own way, find a place in my writing.

To my son Gregg who created my website, *Diannemtarpyauthor.com* and continues to perfect it, I need to publicly say how much I admire your talent and patience. Thank you for buying my first book! I ask many questions, I know. Due to the coaching that you, Eric and Melissa provide, I always arrive at the right, best answer. I cherish the time spent working with all three of you as we do our part in and for our community.

To my photographer friends who provided me inspiration every day, thank you. I shall be indebted to you always for allowing me to use your pictures.

A special mention of thanks to my niece Kerri Spinazola for her photograph of the bay at Bradenton Beach, Florida, which I used as the book cover. It is simply perfect.

At the end of this book, I have included a list of all photos and photographers names used to support the poems contained in this edition. All pictures may be seen aligned with their respective poems on my Facebook or Instagram pages.

Only a few actually appear in this book due to space constraints. My hope is to some day write a book with every poem and its related photo, in color, as it appears on social media.

I would be remiss if I did not include my author/podcast friends whose assistance and encouragement made a difference for me as I published my second book, *A New Day*.

They are: Susana Mueller, owner of Susanasbooks, who created the cover art and supported me graciously and admirably through the formatting steps of the book. It is safe to say I would not have been successful without her professional, capable assistance.

Carolyn Coppola, author of *Minivans, Meltdowns & Merlot*, who provided editing support and cheered me along the way.

The Three Guys Podcast – Brian Nazarian, Brett and Derek DePetrillo, who invited me to participate on their podcast show, and have supported me ever since.

1 - Words Straight from the Heart

"Write it on your heart
that everyday is the best day in the year.
He is rich who owns the day, and no one owns the day
who allows it to be invaded by fret and anxiety.

Finish every day and be done with it
You have done what you could.
Some blunders and absurdities, no doubt crept in.
Forget them as soon as you can, tomorrow is a new day,
begin it well and serenely, with too high a spirit
to be cumbered with your old nonsense.

This new day is too dear,
with its hopes and invitations,
to waste a moment on the yesterdays."
— Ralph Waldo Emerson, Collected Poems and
Translations.

A New Day

This is the beginning. The place that's deep within. Where all my words have meaning, and flow easily off my pen. Each of them begin and end in the heart where the feelings are real. Chapter 1 begins with the poem aptly named Start Where You Are, and then moves on to words that encourage us to listen with intent, and do our part, as we have learned that nobody rides for free.

Dianne M. Tarpy

Start Where You Are

This is what I have learned
The beginning is always today
When you can start over
Again. And Again. And Again.

There should be no feeling of failure
As long as you never give up
Even though you have to start again
Even if the road is long and rocky
Even if you feel as though
you cannot.

I am here to tell you that
Yes, you absolutely can.
I am living proof of this
As here I am again!

My mindset now is different
It is open, positive and moving
Forward is where
Progress is taking me.

Taking the time I need
To appreciate, understand
And be grateful
For all I have achieved.

I know in my heart that
This time
I can definitely be successful
Of this there is no doubt.

Today I shall start where I am
With faith in myself throughout.

Listen to the Wind

Listen to the wind, it speaks.
Listen to the silence and hear
Listen to your heart, it knows.

The wind will tell you everything
You will ever need to know
Sometimes it is just a breeze
And soft
Other times it is howling
And destructive.

The silence can be deafening
Or sometimes hard to hear
Especially when your ears are closed
And you really do not want to know.

Dianne M. Tarpy

Your heart will always be
The one thing you can trust
That which is tried and true
In life
And upon which you can depend.

It is for this very reason that
Each and every day
You will never regret the suggestion
That to our heart we must always listen
As it is our heart that truly knows.

Life Speaks To Us

*"In every community, there is work to be done. In every nation,
there are wounds to heal. In every heart, there is the power to do it."*
- Marianne Williamson

Life is always speaking to us
And if we believe that this is true
Then the question that it
Begs to ask is
Are we listening?

Listening to what it is saying
The lessons that it offers
The moments that so loudly scream
And those that quietly whisper.

Life can be tough
That we know, each and every day
As surely as the sun rises and sets today
It will do the same tomorrow.

Challenges and obstacles may appear
The day gives us much time to do our work
Enough time to heal our wounds
Understanding we have the power
Deep within our hearts.

So, start the day by taking pause
To listen to those things
That life is telling us over and over
Again. And Again. And Again.

Dianne M. Tarpy

Simply Be Willing

Another Monday Morning.
As the fog burns off the land
It is a new beginning.

As we start, yet again, to do those things that are
important,
We must remember:
Yes, we can.

Today is the day.
Simply be willing.
It has nothing to do with being ready.

Often times we are never really ready:
To start that exercise.
To lose those extra pounds
To accomplish that task
Which seems too hard.

Dianne M. Tarpy

The first step in beginning anything
is to simply know these truths:
you are willing
you are able
you can.

After that, anything is possible.
Create that open mindset that
Will lead you towards success.
Simply be willing
Then do your very best.

Live A More Positive Life

What can we do
To live a more positive life?
These times have been challenging
At times it has been difficult to
Remain positive and calm.

Much has to do with our mindset
And ability to align our thoughts
Towards appreciation, gratefulness
At the bounty life presents.

As thoughts affect our actions
And how we as humans react,
Our point of view reflects positively
Or negatively on the path we choose to walk.

We must continue on and keep our thoughts
As positive as possible
For we will find that dwelling on the
Negative is not the place to be
We can all do much better
Residing in the realm of positivity.

Focused, Deliberate Intent

I know I get what I focus on
So today will be the day
I will focus on what I want
That which is most important to my
Life and to my heart.

"Starting strong will change my day
Ending strong will change my life."

This has become a mantra which
Will help me win the day.
Being enthusiastic at the
Start of every single day helps me to
Focus on good habits and the
Dreams I have firmly set in place.

"Continue on," I tell myself with
Focused, deliberate intent
Forward is where I am headed
Knowing I am on to something big
That will change my life forever.

Do Your Part

My ship has arrived!
It's waiting at the dock
Expecting me to board any time
All that is needed
Is for me to believe that
I have earned the right to this moment.

Each day that we live, know this is so,
Our efforts and our actions
Are quite enough
To be wherever we want
And move forward in life
Experiencing all it has to offer.

If we put in the work required
Gain experience and knowledge, too,
Doing all that is right as we
Gain the momentum needed
Our ticket will be punched and ready
For a ride on the sea called life.

Move forward with the feeling
All is well within our heart
What It takes is that simple action
We call - always -
Do your part.

Nobody Rides For Free

We all have our stories.
If we are lucky
The baggage isn't too heavy.

What I have learned is that
Nobody rides for free.

The feelings
The heartache
The sadness
The loneliness
The grief
all becomes part of our being.

They are real.
These feelings.
And they hurt.
Make space for them.
Carry them with you for a while
If you must – then find a place to park them.

Know one thing:
You are not alone.
Nobody rides for free.

2 - The Times of my Life

"In the time of your life, live — so that in that wondrous time you shall not add to the misery and sorrow of the world, but shall smile to the infinite delight and mystery of it. Seek goodness everywhere and when it is found, bring it out of its hiding place and let it be free and unashamed." – William Saroyan – Armenian Short Story writer

Time is the one thing we never get back. Take time to appreciate all that life provides; to celebrate these times as we move through each day. This chapter will explore life, change, choices, and the good in every day. It is through the lens of life that my stories and poems are told. Sometimes a single moment; most often an experience. All share the fact that they are the words that articulate the times of my life, which now have become fond memories.

A New Day

Celebrate All You Have Achieved

Today take time to celebrate
Your growth and gratitude.
As fall approaches
And the beauty of the season unfolds before our eyes
Be thankful.

Reflect on how much our world
Has changed
This is called a year of uncertainty
It really has been tough some days
But, you made it through!

Practice it every day
This ability to work it through
And reach the other side
No matter what life asks of you.
In times of trouble and doubt,
Your mantra is
Yes, I can.

A New Day

Your mind will think
I can do this;
Your lips will say
Continue on.

Re-engage
No matter
How many times it takes
To work it through
Then celebrate
Be grateful and be thankful
For all you have achieved.

Transformation

Much like the dawn of a new day
Slowly transforms our world
Our minds are always thinking
When we look to make a change.

What is your mind trying to tell you?
These are transformative times
In which we live right now, so
Tap into your inner self
And listen to your soul.

Your intuition is speaking loudly
Listen closely with your
Heart and also with your ears
Knowing that the messages
Are important for you to hear.

Be open with your mindset
Know that you are in control
Your wishes are much closer
Than you could ever know.

Continue on your quest to
Seek what's lurking in your mind
Knowing that the transformation
Will take you to whatever
You wish to find.

Sights and Sounds

I have never appreciated the sights and sounds
as much as I do today.

Watching the steam rise from my coffee
the view out my window
the colors of the trees
the sky
the seasons change before me
the birds chirping
the people walking.
the silence.

These times have taught me well.

Where Change Starts

Change starts on the inside

Before we can even begin

We must have an open mindset

To truly expect that we can win.

Enthusiasm will help to overcome

The fear that often stops us from even trying

It is necessary as a motivator

To move forward and make us fly

To those places where success

A New Day

And accomplishment reside.

It is all close within our reach

It is this that I can promise

The transformation within us lies,

Belief and faith of self

Is all that it will take to make change happen

As surely as the sun will rise

Behind the clouds each morning

It is there where change is found

And the transformation begins!

Life's Challenges

Life often presents many challenges

But one thing we must learn

Is to meet those issues head-on

Figure out what you must do

Make a plan to move forward

No matter how hard it may be.

Though the challenges

May be difficult and

Some days easier than others,

Have faith in your ability and the

Fact that you will see it through.

A New Day

Expect barriers and road blocks

Some rocky pathways, too.

Don't let them disappoint you

Take them one by one.

Once you find the solution

There is one thing that you must do

When the moments of

Goodness and gratitude come,

Take the time to rest and relax

Appreciate and be grateful for

All that you have done.

Dianne M. Tarpy

100 Days of Writing
Saturday, June 20, 2020, 100 Days

Thank you, my friends,
(you know who you are)
should I miss a name or two,
for following me the last 100 days
and sharing your
likes and your loves.

Taking the time to read what I wrote
letting me know that you found
worth in the words.
Leaving a comment,
or remark or message
means more than you can ever imagine.

A New Day

You have given me hope
brought a smile to my face
as I worked diligently
to get through
the days.

Your kindness and caring
I will always remember
and for good measure
for you, I have done:

Carved a special place
deep within my heart
as I am
humbled and gratefully touched.
That you took a moment
to read, to like, to love, to comment
my words that came straight from the heart.

As Far As The Eye Can See

I offer you this picture
For it seems to me
We are limited by nothing here
As far as the eye can see.

It is amazing what is available
Open to us everyday
And the best of all is that this view
Is a short ride from my home.

The vastness of the sky and sea
The calming sound of the
Ocean waves
The salty air is a welcome smell
With a breeze that moves softly by.

It is all so very calming
Presented in all its splendor
Asking little in return.

A New Day

One of life's great presents
To be appreciated and revered
To be taken not for granted
Are our many New England Beaches.

They truly are enchanting
And offer much to soothe the soul.
In addition, they are a great analogy
For what we seek in life.

Understanding there are no limits
To what we can attain
When the proper work is put forth
The boxes checked along the way
Even though the path may be rocky
Know that life itself can be limitless
Every opportunity set before us achievable
As far as the eye can see.

Dianne M. Tarpy

Tell Me Something Good Today

Let me hear what made you happy

What turned your frowns to smiles

And made your heart feel good.

Tell me something good today

That you heard about our world,

Your neighbor or your friend,

That finally made you say

"Yes, today is a good day!"

A New Day

And then let's all remember

That there is something in each day

To focus on and be thankful for

Although certainly it is true

That some days are easier than others

To find the something good.

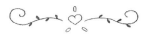

3 - Words of Inspiration and Hope

"A lesson for all of us is that for every loss, there is victory, for every sadness, there is joy, and when you think you've lost everything, there is hope." – Geraldine Solon

These are words of inspiration that have meant to bring you to that place where dreams come true. The intent of this chapter is to help you get there, to that place you want to be. To believe in yourself, know that hope springs eternal, and there is always a glimmer of hope – no matter what.

A New Day

Believe in Yourself

Make your mind go quiet.
Not still.
But quiet now.
Have confidence in your thoughts.

Believe in yourself and
what the day brings
Knowing that belief
it is a powerful tool.

To achieve what you dream of
The first secret to success
Is believing in yourself, for sure.

Create those new habits
That will serve you well
Make today a special day.

Use positive perspectives
That will provide you the motivation
To make yourself healthy
And result in a priceless reward.

Believe in yourself and
Give yourself credit
Never let fear or
The past get in the way.

A New Day

Believe in the truth that
you can and you will
And in the mantra, "Yes, I can."

Do your best always
Love, learn and be happy
It is important to understand

These are the words which will lighten your load and
Serve to illuminate the way
As you begin in this moment
Never to question the power
Believing in yourself can make.

Showing Up

One thing I have learned in life

Is the importance of showing up

Being there when people need you

In good times and in bad.

It is something we remember

Appreciate and love

When someone cares

And takes the time

To be there, no matter what.

So, accept that invitation

Be there when you can

Your caring will be remembered

With love and thankfulness

Showing up is all it took.

Take Action

Today is the day to take action
To move through the day feeling great
Knowing that what actions we take
Will make the difference in our day.

Attitude helps to drive actions
Enthusiasm helps move you faster
Toward that which you hope for
And have set as your goal.

With the right mindset intact,
Hold yourself accountable
For the action you decide to take,

As it is action that will drive
accomplishment and success
And achievement of all of your goals.

Decide to take action today
with a great attitude and enthusiasm as your guides
Knowing the path won't always be easy
Affirming your goals and your thoughts
Striving to be great-not just good-
As good is the enemy of great, they say.

Choose to be great every day!

Dianne M. Tarpy

Hope Springs Eternal

"Hope springs eternal"
We are thankful for those words
As it means that never, ever
Do we have to give up on
What we feel is right and just.

We believe that goodwill happen
That justice will prevail.
It is words like these
That give us hope
That allow us all to know there is
A promised land.

As we begin today, let us be
Inspired to continue on
Doing all the good we can
While knowing we can do better
Then we did yesterday
And say with ultimate confidence
We shall overcome!

A New Day

Have a Past but Don't Live There

Don't get stuck in your ways
Try new things
Venture out
You will be pleasantly surprised.

Make stepping stones
Out of stumbling blocks
Let your past become your guide.

The learning and the experiences
Will help to pave your way
To the achievement and accomplishment
Of all you have ever wanted to become.

Just don't give up.
Move forward!
It is all within your reach.
What is the story that is holding you
Back from life like you wish it to be?

Where Progress May Be Found

It never seems fast enough
It sometimes is very slow
Even though I put in the work
And do all that I am told.

Little by little it is attained
Those goals that I have set
If I am sincere about the effort
Put forth each moment of the day.

I shall practice what is hardest
It is here that opportunity resides
Asking myself this question:
Are my choices helping me
To obtain the progress I seek?

A New Day

It is the path of practice and consistency
That I must walk today
Little by little I shall attain
The progress that is required.

I promise not to complain about
How slow the pace seems to be
Allowing patience and appreciation
To be my friend and my guide

Knowing it is the accumulation
Of my efforts where improvement
And success can ultimately be found.

Work Hard - Dream Big

Dream big
Never give up.

Words of wisdom
That's for sure
That we have all heard before.

What makes them different
Hearing them today
Knowing that, for me,
Today's the day?

The day that I shall
Continue on
No matter what
With no excuses.

A New Day

Though the path
May be sometimes rocky
And the climb often difficult
I shall proceed and move forward.

With an open mindset
That provides the understanding
And the mantra, "Yes, I can."

Today is a new beginning
Knowing I have done it before
I have belief in myself
In my heart and in my head
Realizing I am ready, willing, and able,
More than ever before.

Nothing is Easy

This I have learned.
If it is worth achieving
It usually takes work
And solid determination.

Nothing is easy.
But this I know to be true
There are times that I feel
That I don't have a clue.

But yet, I persist,
In search of what's true.

Nothing is easy
But yet I continue,
"Never give up
Push forward,"
They say.

For it is there where success is waiting.
Where persistence and hard work pay off.

Glimmer of Hope

That's the great thing about hope
It encourages
Inspires
Gives us something to believe in
Even when success seems far away.

It is the belief in the promise of what a new day brings
Possibilities
Opportunities
It is the feeling that everything
Will be okay

Good things will happen
All for the better
That, Yes, I can!

All that is needed is
A glimmer of hope
To push me forward
Accepting that there are some things I can't control
But realizing there is much that
I can.

4 - Blessings Abound

"Concentrate on counting your blessings and you'll have little time to count anything else." – Woodrow Kro

    Blessings may be hidden or right in our own back yard. Often, they are the simple things, right before our eyes. Appreciate and know they have been there forever, just waiting to be found. Living a grateful life helps us to find those blessings. Lighting the way for others helps our own light to burn brighter. May we learn to be a blessing in other's lives as we work together to make this world a better place.

Dianne M. Tarpy

Hidden Blessings

In every trial of life
there is a blessing hidden
but often we must take the time
to open our heart and listen.

Listen to what life is telling us
never knowing quite for sure
what path it will lead us towards
but knowing deep within our hearts
that all of life is a blessing.

Even the trials are worth the time
to be appreciated and learned from;
I suggest you take a moment
to give them thought,
as they are worth addressing.

The cracks we often find
in the road are certainly part of life.
Yet that road, no matter how bumpy,
still gets us where we need to go
and teaches us that nothing is perfect.

So, continue on, no matter what,
on the path that you have chosen;
And know that you were put today
In this very place-
To find the hidden blessings.

Be a Blessing in Somebody's Life

Seek to Make a difference

Help to Lighten the load

Take the burden off their shoulders.

In return

The Karma sent by the universe

Will bring
Peace,
Love,
Joy.

Then

When you least expect it

Yet truly need it

Someone will be a blessing in yours.

Dianne M. Tarpy

Bless and Let it Go

Today I shall find the beauty

In every opportunity that is offered

And give it my best

Being true to myself

As a means to achieving my goals.

I shall bless and let go

All that is not

And be thankful I have a choice.

A New Day

Be the Light

There are times in life that darkness

enters and the light seems very dim,

when even our own candlelight

isn't enough to illuminate the way.

But if we join our light with others

that flame will quickly grow and

the light becomes much brighter

than the sun on a beautiful day.

A New Day

Together we are stronger

than we ever are alone.

Move forward to join with others

combine your light along the way

until that flame is brighter still

and that darkness goes away.

Always be the light for those who share your way.

Have a Mercy

Have mercy....
In a world that seems of late filled
with too much hate
I ask you this:
Have mercy.

Consider the baggage that they may carry
Some stories are sad and break your heart
Some are simply too hard to bear
As certainly life is not always fair
Sometimes it will bring you to your knees.

Know this:
Everyone has a story.
If you are one of the luckier ones that have been given
more than most
I ask you to consider sharing to
Lighten the load if you can.

A New Day

Try to understand the miles they have walked.
Where they are coming from
Along with knowing this:
Some have many roads still left to go.

Doing for others will brighten your day
and make theirs one to remember.

As they say:
"Do All the good you can,
For as long as ever you can."
Please.
Have mercy.

Achievement and Success

No matter how much time
you think that it will take
It usually will take much longer
than you ever could expect
With many obstacles in the way.

But If we see those obstacles
as opportunities
The path to success is easier.

Especially when you realize
That you are never stuck
You are where you choose to be
Continuously convince yourself
That you are in it to win it all.

A New Day

Focus on what's in front today
The most important on your list
Be specific and accountable
to yourself and those around you, too.

Be consistent and at peace
with your journey as you go.

Look for blessings along the way
Realize that consistency is a key
And resilience is required
Knowing that both will help you
find the way where
achievement and success reside.

Dianne M. Tarpy

Listening and Thinking

Experience is the greatest teacher
there are many who would agree
I am inclined to share this view
But I'd like to add two more
I feel are important, too.

I've found that listening to others has given
me an education in itself
And then the resulting questions and answers
are for sure where I have learned.

Thinking is another way that I
have increased my education
It's helped me to realize what things
have served me well and
those that, unfortunately, have not.

A New Day

It is a combination of these two actions,
listening and thinking
That have made such a difference
In my outlook and my knowledge
and the way I see the world.

When added to my formal learning,
(I've earned a few degrees)
I know for sure I am better served
When I stop and take the time to
Listen to other's view points and
to think about all it means.

Karma

"If you lead your life the right way,
the karma will take care of itself". Randy Pausch

I wonder Randy, If you were here today,
what would you call this snow in May? Karma?
Karma because we could do better.
For Mother earth. For our people. For our souls.
Climate change. Is there more to that?
Should we listen closely to those words that ring true?
Is our world suffering more than we know?

It is time.
Time to care about the world and the people who live
here.
Time to be Kind.
To everyone.
To the earth, our family, friends and neighbors.
And those we have yet to meet.
Time to Share.
Didn't Mother tell you it's a nice thing to do?

A New Day

We need to do better. Learn from each other and value
the knowledge that will help us change for the better.
Time to Listen. To nature. To the seas. Our forests
and animals know more than we think. The sun and the
moon provide us the peace that we seek.

How could we not see?
Let's change the Karma.
It is time. Care. Be kind.
Share. Listen.
Live your life the right way.
Take care of our environment.
Let's all do our part.
Our earth and our souls will thank you.

Live your life the right way and the karma will take care
of itself.

Dianne M. Tarpy

Our Blessings

As a society we often stop to count
things we deem important in our life.

Among them are steps, calories, money,
birthdays and breaths we sometimes take.

But what is most important
in this world of ours today

Is to stop and count our
blessings and be thankful
for them all.

For although we are the people
of a nation that has much
uncertainty of late,

We must continue to count the blessings
that are bountiful and true.

These blessings will serve
to keep us hopeful
of all that life has to give
and continue to move us forward

Through life, which is a gift.

5 - Today is a Special Day

"There are only two ways to live your life. One is as though nothing is a miracle. The other is as though everything is a miracle." — Albert Einstein

What is special about today? Most often, it is because we remember, or celebrate a rite of passage; sometimes it is only the promise that a new day will bring; in either case, it should never be underestimated. As we live and breathe to see yet another day, it always starts anew, allowing us the opportunity to experience the best that life has to offer.

A New Day

Dianne M. Tarpy

A Day of Remembering

Monday, May 25, 2020 - Memorial Day
On this day we must remember
those who have paid the price
and gave all they had to give
by making the ultimate sacrifice.

Those who gave their life
so we can live in freedom today
we always shall remember,
with thankfulness and pride.

Soldiers who fought
for God and country,
for service and for self
when all the while
they were fighting
for every one of us.

Dianne M. Tarpy

Today we will be joining
millions of others throughout the world
in a showing of national unity
as we remember our fallen soldiers
Heroes, one and all.

A day we must remember
in the name and honor of
those heroes whose lives were sadly lost;
we will bow our heads to pay homage
before their graves and the grand old flag.

These Heroes are the reason
we celebrate on this day
and why our country
is forever known as the
United States of America's
Home of the free and the brave!

Graduation Day

I shall remember
The feeling of the day.

Riding there in the Jeep
Music blaring. How fun!
The accomplishments
The friendships
The promise that this day offers.

The spirit of happiness that prevailed throughout
knowing it was a job
well done.

Realizing the future is yours.
You've earned your diploma.
The next chapter is about
To begin.

The respect for teachers and administrators;
Those who make a difference each day
And shape the lives of so many students
those who may not even realize the importance
of their contributions
Until many years later in life.

The love and admiration for all
assembled in one place, together.
The laughter.
Family and friends who care.
Celebrating this right of passage.

A sunny day with blue sky
And a slight breeze.
Together throwing the caps into the air.
A fitting tribute. A classic ending.
It couldn't have been any nicer.

I shall remember always your
Graduation day.

Sunday, June 14, 2020

On Flag Day and every day
May we never forget the pride
That goes with viewing the symbol
Of our country far and wide.

A symbol that stands for the freedom
That we all can proudly claim
Due to those who have triumphantly
Fought for us,
Along with self, God and country.

May we always remember that
Nothing comes for free
That many have
Paid the price
To ensure our life and liberty.

May this high flying flag
Of ours forever wave!
Not just for today, but every day
Over the land of the free and the brave!

Mother's Day 2020

Happy Mother's Day!

"It's your Mother who loves you," I often say whenever a call comes in from one of my three kids. I often wonder if they fully realize the depth of those simple words. The amount of true, pure love that comes with that sentiment.

I shall remember always the Mother's Days I've had.

Starting at an early age when Gregg was the first There is nothing that can compare to that first born baby's love. He was the best baby. With a smile that can move mountains. A hard worker, he was loved by everyone.

Then along came Eric. The middle child. His love always rings true. From the time he was very little, he was my quiet one, but always the leader, puts family first, and can be depended on to know what is the right thing to do.

Last, but not least, was my daughter Melissa, who now is a Mother to two beautiful girls, and always makes me proud. Creative, athletic and a never-give-up, yes-I-can daughter who has the bluest of eyes. As a coach she has an impact on many, and works hard to improve their skills. On and off the court.

I'd be remiss if I did not mention the other Mother's that have been important in my life- my own Mom Barbara, who I loved dearly, Jim's Mom Althea, and my Grandmother's, Grammie and Baba. Each played a huge role in shaping my life. For that I am grateful.

To Stacey and Christina, know always how thankful I am to have you in my life; I've watched you grow and become great Mothers. Know always how much you are loved. My grandchildren bring me much joy. Thank you for bringing them into our world!

From a friend whose words truly resonate with me: "Happy Mother's Day to these amazing women, and to all the moms not pictured here who have also touched my life. Happy Mother's Day to those who are trying, who have miscarried, who have lost, who adopt, who foster, who are alone, who are in heaven, and who are motherly figures for so many others. Know that you are loved and appreciated".

When I look back, I realize that I have accomplished much, and I am truly blessed. But what means the most is the job I've held and my calling as Mother. And how my heart swells with pride, not just today on Mother's Day, but also every other, when I hear the words "Hi Mom, how was your day? "It's your Mother who loves you..." I say.

We Shall Think of You

Always smiling.

In later years, even though in pain,

You had a beautiful way about you.

With a mind as sharp as a tack,

You always remembered our birthdays

With a card or a call or both.

Dressed always so nicely

Hair in latest fashion

You were certainly a role model.

Dianne M. Tarpy

For what 90 years of good

living, life and loving

Should look like.

As we celebrate your life today

May you forever know that

It is with love and admiration
Held deep within our hearts.

We shall think of you.

Rest In Peace Aunt Madeline.
May God hold you always in the Palm of His hand.

Happy Father's Day

"It's just another day," he says
Of this I can be sure
In this one case I know he's wrong
Because today is Father's Day!

Jim and Gregg and Eric
Examples one and all
Of what it means to be the best
Papa, Dad's and role models.
Always there, no matter what
The three of them are quite alike
We can always count on them
To do what's right, to love us all,
Accomplish just what's needed.

Handymen,
They have the knowledge
and the tools in the garage
To fix anything that's looking bad or broke,
or simply needs updating.

Dianne M. Tarpy

Working hard their entire lives
Along with cooking, cleaning or doing wash,
(They are capable of all three)
Steady, firm and true;
kind to not just their family's
But to the community too.

We are indeed certainly blessed
That I know for sure,
After witnessing their accomplishments
through these many years;

So it is with pride and admiration
I proclaim today and every day
That no one could be prouder of
These three guys you see pictured here.

A New Day

Half a Year

Six months gone
2020 has been quite a year
Will we ever forget?
So much uncertainty.
Fear and anxiety
have been the norm.
It's time to start to turn it around.

Begin with change
That is positive and true.
Breaking bad habits
And starting anew.
"Yes, I can!"
Shall be our mantra
Continuing on, moving forward.

Taking action now will help
To make our dreams come true.
Make the next 6 months of 2020 be
The best for you and your family
Turn it Into a year of positivity
Forget the bad, but learn from it
Believe in the good
and make it work.

Dianne M. Tarpy

Sportsmanship

"I've got your back no matter what,
I believe in you."
Are there any words
That mean more than that
When we are a member of a team?

The score's important, that we know
But win or lose
We will always learn
One thing or another
That serves to make us better
Team members and human beings.

Good sportsmanship will carry on
No matter what the age
From high school into college and even far beyond
As we move into the business world
As grownups with a job
Teamwork and belief in others
Will always be the key
To success and accomplishment,
For individuals and teams.

Dianne M. Tarpy

Words in Honor of Bradford Swim Club 2020
sportsmanship award winners
Presented on August 14, 2020, by Dianne Tarpy, Sponsor,
to: Jack LaPierre, Naomi McLaughlin, Palmer Randall, and
Tyler Tarpy.

6 - Grateful for this Moment

"Sometimes our light goes out but is blown again into instant flame by an encounter with another human being. Each of us owes the deepest thanks to those who have rekindled this inner light." – Albert Schweitzer

Living with a full heart. I have never fully realized the beauty and joy that gratitude offers. It has been only when I stop and pause to reflect on simple things that I find them, those things I often took for granted. Encountering and working with people who care fosters a feeling of true awareness for ourselves and others. In turn, we become grateful for each moment. This awareness leads to a life of happiness.

Dianne M. Tarpy

Grateful

A back yard picture this morning.
Coffee and muffins on the deck.
Can anything mean more these days
Then a quick visit from your son?

Or yesterday when chicken salads appear
Without even asking
And lunch is taken care of
Thanks to the kindness of your son?

Or when the call comes in
I am at the store, send me your list
Exactly when the time is right and when you have a need.

How does your daughter always seem to know?
While these may be the simple things that
many take for granted, I shall be forever grateful to
Gregg, Eric and Melissa -and their families- for their
kindness always. Especially during these extraordinary
times.

A New Day

Dianne M. Tarpy

Today YES, I CAN!

Here we go.
Today's the day!

As I stop and take a moment
To figure out what I can do
To make life even better
I think about the need to be consistent in all I do.

It is the "Yes, I can" mentality
that will help achieve my goals
And also facing the reality
that it is really all up to me.

What one improvement can I make
That makes today better than yesterday?
Today I shall align my thoughts with
what I truly want the most.

A New Day

Returning to the now with things
Because yesterday and the past
Matters not in the scheme of things.
I am finally on my way.

With an open mindset
and eyes looking towards success,
the affirmation stated simply,
"Yes, I can," planted firmly in my head
I shall be moving forward
working hard to win the day!

Dianne M. Tarpy

The Flames of a Fire

Are beautiful, especially at night
How I love to watch the glow
As the fire dances back and forth
and warms us as we sit.

It is a thing of beauty
When under a watchful eye
For you see my son and grandson are firefighter's
And have taught us to make sure it is safe.

A fire is much like life;
It must be prepared,
treated with care and patience,
and protected by those who surround it
While given space and
room to flourish.
It is then we will feel the warmth.

Always be a Beginner

Keep your mind ready and open
To learn all you can
No matter what the topic.

For the minute you think
You know it all
Is the moment
when the real work begins.

Keep your mind empty.
An empty and ready mind
Is in all ways ready for everything
Anything becomes possible.

Never stop learning
Don't limit yourself
Or your ideas
Keep your mind fresh
Always be a beginner.

Dianne M. Tarpy

Another Day

Here we are.

Again.

Blue sky.

Beautiful day.

How will we use it?

To further our goals.

To make a difference

In our life or someone else's.

Each of us has the power within

and can decide.

Use this day wisely

Make it count

For it will never come again.

Harness the Power

The sun
The moon
The stars
Are here for you each day.
Moment by moment
Choice by choice
It is our destiny to choose
That which best suits our needs
What is it you seek?
Good health?
Happiness?
Joy?
It is ours to choose.
Choose wisely.
May we never take for granted
the simple things in life.
And the power we have to choose.

Dianne M. Tarpy

Here, All is Right With the World

The open sky
The water blue
The ocean breeze
The brilliant sun
The smell of the salt air
Will never leave my mind.
These majestic views
And smells
Warm my heart.
It is by the sea I want to be
With waves crashing
The water making its own rhythm
Helping to arrange my thoughts.
It clears my head
And helps me to understand
The blessings rolled out before me
The expanse of the sky and sea
Provides me the lens through
which I see that here,
all is right with the world.

I Can

On this day

I choose optimism

In the face of all the negativity

All the pessimistic thoughts

The bad press

Today I will choose the positive,

Optimistic perspective of life

Realizing that I am in control

Of my thoughts and actions

And that, on this day, I can.

Continue On

Each day is precious

But we often take it for granted.

To you I promise:

I will do my best
To love
To laugh
To take advantage
Of all things we are given.

And be thankful.

7 - Living a Life of Peace

"Never be in a hurry; do everything quietly and in a calm spirit. Do not lose your inner peace for anything whatsoever, even if your whole world seems upset." - Saint Francis de Sales

Living a life of stillness and peace is a blessing. As we make choices and promises to ourselves and each other, we bring ourself back to that place of peace where all is right in our world. May we seek always to find that place where peace resides.

A New Day

Peace

May today you find peace in the rain

Peace in your hearts

Peace in your thoughts

And be thankful.

Choices and Promises

Shine your light.
You never know when
it will help someone
get through the storm.

Share your knowledge
In hopes that it will make it
Easier for those behind you.

Shape the world in which you live
Help the world to keep its promises
Start with yourself
One day, one promise at a time.

As today begins, know you
can and will make a difference.
Your choices and promises
-those made to ourselves & others-

Will shape a world
in which light shines and
 knowledge, once shared,
will create and promote
a world of happiness and
peace for all.

Dianne M. Tarpy

Life Differently

Can we?
Do life differently?
If we have learned nothing
During the pandemic
Perhaps we are smarter.

What are our greatest gifts?
I have learned.
These times have taught us much.

The importance of good health
And knowing what we must do to stay healthy,

The importance of being grateful
And sharing this with our world

Dianne M. Tarpy

The importance of being humble and kind
Knowing we are one of many who search for them daily.

These times have taught us
we are not alone in our quest for
Love, happiness and joy
Even in these darkest of times
Understanding they are the keys to a good life.

Can we do life differently?
Can we use our greatest gifts
to help ourselves and others?
Have these times taught us nothing?
Can we do life differently?
Only you can know.

The Voice that Matters

The voice that matters
Is yours.

Train your mind
And your heart
To see the good
In all you do.

As your journey begins,
Empty your mind of all thoughts;
allow your heart to be at peace.

Let the knowledge you have accumulated be your guide.
Listen to that voice in your head
Let it be the
One that you follow.

You know best.
Upon yourself you can depend.
Check in on your heart.
Cultivate the stillness and purpose
Peace and clarity
That will bring you to the place
you have always wanted to be.

Listen to your voice. It matters.

Dianne M. Tarpy

Be Sure to Watch

I cannot believe that this beech tree sprouted leaves
practically overnight
Even though I have been watching for it
It happened right before my eyes.

It made me think about many things
Like the fact that my children have grown
And made me proud
Then had children of their own.

My grandchildren are my pride and joy
Each one more precious than the other
There now are eight, I've watched them grow
I know that I am blessed.

Dianne M. Tarpy

The years go by and life moves on
More quickly than expected
Enjoy these days and use them well
There are no guarantees.

Enjoy the moments that life provides
And find joy in those simple things
Seek peace wherever it may dwell.

Be kind. Love often. Live well .
Be sure to watch, because you'll see
Often it is over before you know it
Even though
It is right before your eyes.

Be sure to watch.

Simplicity

If only life could be
As simple as a daisy
Not complicated at all
It would make our days
More peaceful
With less stress to be endured.

If we could simplify our being
And bring peace unto our life
How much easier it would be
To lay down upon the pillow
At the end of every day.

Remember the simplicity of a daisy,
Which grows abundantly in the ground,
And know it's best to keep it simple
when life gets hard to handle
As it's there that peace is found.

Find that Place

The place where peace is living
Where everything seems brand new
Where you can start again
To do what you want to do
Where sunshine and blue sky
Along with sparkling water, too
Are there free for the taking
Where dreams are clear
Thoughts are pure
Where stillness and the quiet
Bring you joy and happiness
Take time to celebrate the fact
That you are more than enough
Be proud of what that means
Find that place
Keep it close
In your heart and in your mind.

A New Day

Stop

Stop and take a moment
to be without your phone
it is actually amazing
how liberating it can be.

We think we really need it every
moment of the day when truly we can
go without and suffer no consequences.

Most of us get anxious
if we lose or are separated from the device.
I actually saw a study that said it is as high as 66%.
Let me offer some advice:
It has almost become an addiction and
drug of choice for many.

They are even measuring weekly screen time
now and telling us if we are up or down.

While I know I am not the first to say
I could never go without it
let me tell you here and now
try it -stop-go without it for a day.
I think you'll find you like it
For the peace that it provides
And the quiet it delivers.

Dianne M. Tarpy

Stillness and Peace

Where o'art thou do we find thee?
In this troubled world of ours
The benefits of
Stillness and peace
Enough to quiet the mind
And find the calm we seek?
Shall we begin the day with a strong belief?
And a quiet stillness within
That will serve us well
Throughout the entire day
On this, can we depend?
Everyday gives us another chance
Filled with unlimited possibilities
We must find that path
that serves us best
shine a light upon ourselves
It is there that we will find that special place where
new life and calm reside
a new day
that brings us
stillness and peace
happiness and love.

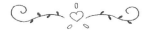

8 - Love will Bring us Together

"The very center of your heart is where life begins. The most beautiful place on earth." — Rumi, The Love Poems of Rumi

The love we have for each other reminds us that every moment together is special and every second should be cherished. It is the never-ending circle of life that's filled with love. This love is as necessary as the air we breathe in order to prosper and grow. Love is needed to achieve the success we search for in our life.

A New Day

Three Things

"Only three things can change our life; dreams, suffering, and love." - Paulo Coelho

Today I'd ask you to think. Think of the changes we've gone through in the past 58 days.

Think of all the dreams that have died; and of those that have grown.

Think of all the things that now are different. Some for the better, some for the worse.

Think of all the suffering you've seen, heard or read about. Or had to experience.

The one thing that has stayed consistent throughout all these days is love.
It is love that pulls us through all situations. Whether good or bad. The love of self, or the dreams we have in our heart.

The love of family and friends, the love of the greater good.
Love.
Every.
Single.
Time.

A New Day

How Can You Make a Difference Today?

What can you do to lighten someone's load?

Giving from the goodness of one's heart
is rewarding as we can see the direct impact.

It is in giving that we receive
When one only will believe
In the difference that
their actions can make for themselves and others
whose path they may take.

Feel and share gratitude and praise
For the simple things in life
Believe in the beauty each day can bring
Along with those things we choose to give
to others as we go along our way:

A smile
An encouraging word
A hug
Brings us laughter and love.

Focus on all the good
That you can do
One person can make a difference, you see
Making the world better
For you.
For me.

The Journey

Embrace the journey.
Let it take you away
To the place you want to be
With hard work and discipline
The world is at your feet.

Continue on even when it is tough
Because on the other side
Is the place you have dreamed of
Where the life you always imagined
is close within your grasp
Exactly as you wish it to be.

No one ever promised
us a rose garden
But this I know is true
Perseverance here is key.

For as sure as the sun rises
each morning
We can have a life that is filled
With peace, love and happiness
If we take responsibility
for writing our own story
Embracing the journey in all its glory
No matter what life presents.

The Value of Life Spent Together

Is never fully realized
until the time is over
And then it becomes firmly implanted
In our minds as a memory.

As the years are passing quickly
(This I know for sure)
I am thankful for every
Opportunity that is offered to me now.

An invitation I shall
Always take
because these
Times are precious, you see;
Meaning more and more to me
As each single minute passes.

These memories I shall forever keep
Together In my heart and mind
As they shall always be to me
One more valuable than the other.

Live your Life as you Believe

Doing the things you know
Are good
For yourself
For your family.
For your community.

Share your gifts
With those who will benefit
Teach what you have learned
To the world.

Be confident.
Knowing that
In giving you will
receive back more than tenfold.

In the end, your legacy
Will stand the rest of time
You will be remembered
For the good you have done
And your love that has endured.

A New Day

Grief

There are times in life
when grief hits hard.
When losing someone
Comes quickly we are marred
By the loss of love
And companionship.

Then the memories come
Floating in and they help to
Take some of the sting away
Remembering the good times
We had together.
The laughter
The comfort
The love.

A New Day

This grief and the pain it causes
Never ends.
But it does change.
It is a place we pass through.
This feeling is not one of weakness.
Nor is it a lack of faith.
But, as they say,
It is the price we pay for love.

To love and be loved deeply
Is one of life's greatest treasures.
Rest easy my friend.
Knowing how deeply
you were loved.
Know that I shall see you in the sun
That rises every single day
And as it sets, you will be there, too
In my mind and in my heart
Forever you will stay.

Dianne M. Tarpy

I Will Always Hold a Lantern

For you.
No matter what the weather
Come rain and fog or snow
Sun and bright
Day or night.
I will
Be here for you.
I will hold your hand and listen
Or give advice
Or cry along with you.
I can do that, too.
Just know deep in your heart
I will always hold a lantern for you.

Our World

It is sad at the moment.
Our world is falling apart.
It needs our help.
What can we do?

We must take the steps
As necessary to make the
World a better place.
A smile, a good deed
Here and there may well be
All that it takes;

Be generous with what
We have been given,
Sharing whatever we make.

Find ways to fall in love with life
Even though at times it's tough
Our world of late is not a pretty one
As it seems there is too much hate.

If each of us can do our part
In our respective communities
However small the gesture
If it makes a positive difference
In our world and in our life
At least it is a start and a welcome one
To make our world a better place.

Take Time

Take time to invite
Stillness into your life
It is there that solitude is found
Solitude is that place where
You can feed your soul
And think about what's important.

Take time to turn your dreams into plans and
Think about the action you will take.
Resisting the comparison game,
Do what makes you happy.

You can't compare the
Sun and moon
They shine when it is their time.
Take time to find the place where
Joy, love and happiness reside
Along with purposeful,
Interesting work.

Stay close to family, friends and
Those who love you most, as
It is that place that you will find
A life well lived
Where all your dreams come true.

Epilogue

If my book *A New Day* makes a difference in one person's life, helping them to move swiftly, and confidently through the day, I have achieved my goal.

It is my wish that these words of inspiration, in this my second book in the series of *From the Heart,* will bring hope, understanding, and healing to the world.

About the Author

Dianne M. Tarpy, the author of *From the Heart*, worked in the corporate telecommunications environment for over 34 years. In this role, she experienced first-hand the life-altering tragedy of 9/11 in New York City and the resulting aftermath and restoration of the network. She is a community and family-focused leader, resident, and hometown sports fan from Haverhill, Massachusetts, where she has lived her entire life. As a wife, mother of three, and Nana to eight beautiful grandchildren, she has lived long enough to experience life at its best and its worst. Having achieved two master's degrees, she is the recipient of a number of awards at the national and local level for her work achieved in giving back to the community in which she lives and works. A voracious, lifelong reader, writing has always come easy. Little did she know that lying quietly within her were books waiting to be written - she just needed the right time and mental space to do so. The silver lining of the pandemic is that she feels as though her life's purpose has been realized. She believes in learning that never ends and knows that one person can – and does – make a difference. As well as knowing that it is never too late to do or be all that you wish for.

Credits

Index of Titles and First Lines

Made in the USA
Columbia, SC
14 July 2021

41826956R00080